The Plus and Minus Of Social Media in 2024

Social media, a ubiquitous term in today's digital age, traces its roots back to the early days of the internet and has since evolved into a powerful force that shapes our interactions, influences our behaviors, and impacts our lives in profound ways.

Understanding the origins, benefits, and dangers of social media provides a comprehensive view of its complex role in modern society.

The Origins of Social Media

The concept of social media isn't entirely new.

It can be traced back to early forms of digital communication like bulletin board systems (BBS) and internet relay chat (IRC) in the late 1970s and early 1980s.

These platforms allowed users to connect and share information in a rudimentary form, laying the groundwork for more sophisticated networks.

In the mid-1990s, the advent of the World Wide Web brought about the first recognizable social media sites.

Websites like GeoCities (1994) and Classmates.com (1995) enabled users to create personal web pages and reconnect with old friends.

However, it was the launch of Six Degrees in 1997 that truly marked the beginning of social networking.

Six Degrees allowed users to create profiles, list their friends, and surf the friend lists. Despite its eventual shutdown in 2001, Six Degrees highlighted the potential of connecting people online.

The early 2000s saw the rise of several influential social media platforms.

Friendster (2002), MySpace (2003), and LinkedIn (2003) each introduced unique features that catered to different user needs, from personal expression and music sharing to professional networking.

However, it was the launch of Facebook in 2004 that revolutionized social media.

Initially limited to Harvard students, Facebook's expansion to other universities and eventually to anyone over 13 with an email address transformed it into a global phenomenon.

Twitter, launched in 2006, introduced the concept of microblogging, allowing users to share short updates, or "tweets," and rapidly gain followers.

Instagram (2010), Snapchat (2011), and TikTok (2016) further diversified the social media landscape with their focus on visual content, ephemeral messages, and short-form videos, respectively.

Each platform built on its predecessors' successes and introduced new features that resonated with users, driving the rapid evolution of social media.

The Benefits of Social Media

Social media offers a myriad of benefits that have reshaped the way we communicate, connect, and consume information.

Connectivity and Communication:

Social media bridges geographical distances, enabling people to stay connected with friends and family worldwide.

Platforms like Facebook, WhatsApp, and Instagram facilitate instant communication through messages, photos, and videos, fostering a sense of closeness even when physically apart.

Information and Awareness:

Social media serves as a powerful tool for disseminating information and raising awareness about various issues.

Twitter's real-time updates, for instance, have made it a go-to source for breaking news, while platforms like Instagram and Facebook allow users to share stories and campaigns, amplifying voices that might otherwise go unheard.

Community Building:

Social media enables the formation of communities based on shared interests, hobbies, and causes.

From niche Facebook groups to subreddit forums, users can find and engage with like-minded individuals, creating a sense of belonging and support.

Professional Networking:

LinkedIn has transformed professional networking by providing a platform for job seekers, employers, and professionals to connect, share their expertise, and advance their careers.

It facilitates job searches, recruitment, and professional development, making it an invaluable tool in the modern job market.

Marketing and Business Growth:

Social media has revolutionized marketing and advertising.

Businesses can reach a global audience, engage with customers directly, and promote their products or services through targeted ads and influencer partnerships. Platforms like Instagram and Facebook offer robust tools for businesses to build brand awareness and drive sales.

Creativity and Self-Expression:

Social media platforms provide outlets for creativity and self-expression.

Instagram and TikTok, for example, enable users to share their artistic endeavors, from photography and art to music and dance, with a wide audience.

This democratization of content creation has given rise to countless influencers and content creators.

Educational Opportunities:

Social media is a valuable resource for learning and education.

YouTube offers tutorials on virtually any subject, while platforms like Twitter and LinkedIn host discussions and webinars on industry trends and innovations.

Educational institutions also use social media to engage with students and share information.

The Dangers of Social Media

Despite its numerous benefits, social media also poses significant dangers that can have adverse effects on individuals and society.

Privacy Concerns:

Social media platforms collect vast amounts of personal data, raising concerns about privacy and data security.

Breaches and unauthorized access to personal information can lead to identity theft, financial loss, and other security issues.

Mental Health Issues:

Excessive use of social media has been linked to mental health problems such as anxiety, depression, and loneliness.

The constant comparison to others' curated lives, cyberbullying, and the pressure to maintain a perfect online persona can negatively impact self-esteem and well-being.

Addiction and Time Management:

Social media can be highly addictive, leading to excessive screen time and neglect of real-life responsibilities.

The dopamine-driven feedback loops of likes, comments, and shares can create a compulsion to stay connected, disrupting productivity and sleep patterns.

Misinformation and Fake News:

The rapid spread of misinformation and fake news on social media platforms can have serious consequences, from influencing public opinion to inciting violence.

Algorithms that prioritize sensational content can amplify false information, making it difficult for users to discern the truth.

Echo Chambers and Polarization:

Social media can create echo chambers where users are exposed only to information and opinions that align with their own.

This can reinforce biases, deepen divisions, and contribute to political and social polarization.

Cyberbullying and Harassment:

The anonymity and reach of social media can facilitate cyberbullying and harassment.

Victims of online abuse can experience severe emotional distress, leading to long-term psychological effects.

Impact on Relationships:

While social media can enhance communication, it can also strain relationships.

Misunderstandings, jealousy, and the constant availability of alternative connections can lead to conflicts and diminished intimacy in personal relationships.

Influence on Behavior and Perception:

Social media can influence behavior and shape perceptions, sometimes in harmful ways.

The promotion of unrealistic beauty standards, risky behaviors, and materialism can affect users' self-image and lifestyle choices.

Balancing Benefits and Dangers

Navigating the benefits and dangers of social media requires a balanced approach.

Awareness and proactive measures can help mitigate the risks while maximizing the advantages.

Privacy Settings and Data Protection:

Users should regularly review and adjust their privacy settings to control who can access their information.

Being mindful of the data shared online and using strong passwords can enhance security.

Mindful Usage:

Setting boundaries and limiting screen time can prevent social media addiction and its negative effects on mental health.

Designating specific times for social media use and engaging in offline activities can promote a healthier balance.

Critical Thinking and Media Literacy:

Developing critical thinking skills and media literacy is essential for navigating the information landscape on social media.

Users should verify sources, question the credibility of content, and be wary of sensationalism.

Supporting Positive Interactions:

Encouraging positive interactions and standing against cyberbullying can foster a more supportive online environment.

Reporting abusive behavior and offering support to those affected can make a difference.

Promoting Mental Health:

Seeking help when needed and promoting mental health awareness can mitigate the negative impact of social media on mental well-being.

Platforms can also contribute by implementing features that promote positive interactions and mental health resources.

Diversifying Information Sources:

To avoid echo chambers, users should seek out diverse perspectives and engage with content from various sources.

This can broaden understanding and reduce polarization.

The Future of Social Media

As technology continues to advance, the future of social media will likely see further innovations and challenges.

Emerging technologies like artificial intelligence, virtual reality, and augmented reality have the potential to transform how we interact with social media.

Conclusion

Social media, with its deep-rooted origins in the early days of the internet, has become an integral part of modern life.

From the pioneering platforms of the late 1990s to today's sophisticated networks, social media has revolutionized how we communicate, share information, and engage with the world.

Its benefits are vast, enabling connectivity, fostering communities, supporting businesses, and democratizing information.

However, these advantages come with significant dangers, including mental health issues, privacy concerns, cyberbullying, misinformation, and societal polarization.

Balancing the benefits and dangers of social media is crucial for navigating the digital landscape responsibly.

Digital literacy and education are paramount in helping users understand how to protect their privacy, recognize misinformation, and maintain healthy online habits.

Encouraging positive content and promoting critical thinking can help create a more constructive and empathetic online environment.

Looking ahead, emerging technologies like virtual reality, augmented reality, and artificial intelligence will continue to evolve social media, offering new ways to interact and experience the digital world.

However, these advancements will also bring new challenges, such as privacy and security concerns, which will need careful consideration.

Decentralized social networks and thoughtful regulation may provide solutions to some of the current issues, giving users more control over their data and holding platforms accountable for harmful content.

As society continues to grapple with the complexities of social media, finding a balance between leveraging its benefits and mitigating its risks will be essential for ensuring that it remains a force for good in our lives.

By fostering a more informed, responsible, and positive online culture, we can harness the power of social media to enrich our personal and collective experiences while safeguarding against its potential harms.

Please use the next few pages for your notes and debates.

www.ingramcontent.com/pod-product-compliance
Lightning Source LLC
Chambersburg PA
CBHW072019230526
45479CB00008B/296